CYBER GROOMING: UNDERSTANDING THE THREAT IN THE DIGITAL WORLD

DR DHEERAJ MEHROTRA

Contents

Preface

It is a luxury and a duty to traverse the infinite possibilities of the internet world today when the digital environment affects our lives so profoundly. The internet facilitates communication, expands our horizons academically and culturally, and provides endless entertainment options. Yet, amid this vast domain of connectedness, there emerges a murky menace that preys on innocence, abuses trust, and shatters lives—a peril known as cyber grooming.

*This book, "**Cyber Grooming: Understanding the Threat in the Digital World**," aims to shed light on the hidden places on the internet where predators operate, to expose the methods they use, and to equip individuals, families, educators, and communities with the information they need to counteract this pervasive threat.*

Through the following pages, we will go on a trip into the heart of cyber grooming, exploring its nuances, its victims' tales, and the measures we may take to safeguard ourselves and those we care about. The emotional toll of grooming and the motivations of those who prey on the weak in the digital sphere will be revealed.

In addition to being a wealth of information, this book also serves as a rallying cry. It's an appeal to break the hush around cyber grooming and encourage more open dialogue about the risks of the internet. It's a call to action to educate ourselves and our children about the benefits and drawbacks of social media and other internet platforms. It promises to help those who have survived trauma get back on track.

We need to step up to the job of countering this digital threat. We must learn to think critically and act decisively to protect our online communities. There has to be an environment where people feel secure speaking out about their problems. We must work together to stop cyberbullying and make the web safer for everyone.

I hope you'll read this book with an open heart and a sharp mind as we embark on our journey together. A better, more secure digital world where trust is earned, innocence is maintained, the light of information dispels the darkness, and awareness is within our reach if we work together to decipher the subtleties of cyber grooming and shine a light on its dark corners.

I am grateful for coming along on this essential trip.

Author

ONE
INTRODUCTION

The Information Age: Both Opportunities and Dangers

We begin our trip into the heart of the digital era in the first chapter of "Cyber Grooming: Understanding the Threat in the Digital World," which takes us into a period of extraordinary connectedness and invention. Even though the digital world presents exceptional chances for communication, education, and development, it also carries a sinister and covert danger known as cyber grooming.

What exactly does "Cyber Grooming" mean?

To begin, we will define the word "cyber grooming," which may seem foreign to some people but is essential to understand in the context of protecting oneself when using the internet. The term "cyber grooming" refers to the predatory practice of adults, often with nefarious intentions, forming connections online with children and teenagers. Deception, manipulation, and the slow but steady taking advantage of weak prey are the foundations for these relationships.

The Repercussions for the Victims

This chapter highlights the significant repercussions cyberbullying may have on the individuals who fall prey to it. Its effects are not confined to the here and now; instead, it leaves permanent scars, both psychologically and emotionally. The results of being groomed may significantly impact a victim's life, including their sense of self-worth, ability to trust people, and general well-being.

We examine the experiences of those who have been victimized by online grooming, highlighting the need to understand the scope of the damage inflicted and the pressing need to find a solution to this problem as quickly as possible. These accounts serve as a jarring reminder that the issue of cyber grooming is not an abstract one; instead, it is something that may happen to anybody at any time, in any location.

The Value of Being Aware of Something

The need for awareness and education as the

first lines of protection against cyber grooming is emphasized. Individuals can take preventative measures to safeguard themselves and the people they care about by first identifying the warning signals and red flags that indicate potential danger.

The world of computers is a significant and complicated environment, and cyber grooming is one of the hidden dangers that lurk inside it. As we go further into the following chapters, we will uncover the strategies that groomers use, investigate real-life tales, and give practical recommendations on preventing sexual assault, reporting incidents, and recovering from sexual assault.

Knowledge is power in the face of this danger posed by digital technology. We can get a head start on the critical task of protecting the next generation of digital natives and building an online environment that is less dangerous and more secure for everyone if we have a solid grasp of the terrain and the dynamics of cyber grooming.

TWO

THE GROOMING PROCESS

The Strategies of the Groomer, the Weaknesses of the Victim, and the Development of the Grooming Process

In Chapter 2 of "Cyber Grooming: Understanding the Threat in the Digital World," we delve further into the troubling realm of online grooming by studying the complex process that groomers use to abuse their victims.

This chapter is a part of a book titled "Cyber Grooming: Understanding the Threat in the Digital World."

Deception and manipulation are the tools of the groomer's trade.

This chapter will begin by analyzing the strategies that groomers use. Groomers are skilled in creating online personalities that give the impression of being reliable and approachable. They often assume the identities of peers, mentors, or sympathetic persons who seem to provide their targets with friendship, compassion, and support to deceive them. It is necessary to understand these strategies to identify possible dangers in the digital environment and protect yourself from them.

The Vulnerabilities of the Victim and Establishing Trust

The success of a groom depends on the groom's ability to recognize and take advantage of their victim's weak spots. Challenges a young person may be confronting on an emotional, psychological, or social level might be examples of existing vulnerabilities. This chapter examines groomers' methods to exploit these weaknesses to win their victims' confidence and control them further. Groomers try to persuade their targets to think they are trustworthy and reliable friends by acting sympathetic and compassionate toward their targets.

The Unsettling Truth Behind the Development of Grooming

As we go further in the chapter, we will dig more into the sneaky nature of the grooming process. The grooming process often involves being slow and meticulous. The first step for groomers is to establish rapport and trust with their clients before progressively raising the bar regarding their expectations. Victims can find themselves caught in a loop of emotional manipulation and compulsion, which makes it more difficult for them to break free from the grip of the groomer.

The need to be vigilant and attentive throughout the process of recognizing grooming activities and possible dangers is emphasized in Chapter 2. It underscores the need for open talks with young people about their experiences online, building an atmosphere in which they feel secure discussing any concerns or suspicions.

Readers acquire valuable insights into the strategies groomers use and the weaknesses that make persons vulnerable to grooming if they grasp the process by which grooming occurs. With this information, we can take preventative measures to safeguard ourselves and the people we care about from falling prey to the ever-present danger lurking in the digital sphere.

In the following chapters, we will continue our discussion of the warning signals and red flags of grooming, as well as the real-life experiences of survivors, various preventative techniques, and the critical role that education and support play in the fight against cyberbullying.

THREE
SIGNS AND RED FLAGS

Objective: Recognizing Grooming Behaviors, Figuring Out Who Might Be Vulnerable, and Keeping an Eye on Any Changes in Behaviour

The third chapter of "Cyber Grooming: Understanding the Threat in the Digital World" dives into detecting the indications and warning flags related to online grooming. To safeguard oneself and others from possible damage in the digital sphere, it is vital to maintain a state of vigilance and observation at all times.

Identifying Certain Grooming Behaviors

The first part of this chapter is dedicated to enlightening the readers about groomers' numerous actions. These actions may include excessive flattery, secrecy, efforts to isolate the victim, and manipulation via guilt or fear. Other examples of these behaviours include trying to isolate the victim. By gaining an awareness of these strategies, people might improve their ability to recognize when they may be the target of someone else's effort to groom them.

Locating Potentially Vulnerable Targets

Another important topic covered in this chapter is identifying those individuals who are most likely to be victimized by groomers online. Vulnerabilities may take many forms, such as poor self-esteem, loneliness, or a robust want for recognition and affirmation. When prospective victims and support networks know their vulnerabilities, they can take preventative actions to safeguard themselves against exploitation.

Keeping an Eye on How Behaviour Changes

As the process of grooming continues, victims often see observable changes in their behaviour and attitude. These changes could include isolating themselves from their family and friends, being more secretive about their activity online, and experiencing increasing mental anguish. Parents, guardians, and friends can take immediate action to intervene and give support if they remain sensitive to the changes in their child's behaviour.

Trust and Open Lines of Communication

The necessity of honest communication and the cultivation of trust is underlined throughout Chapter 3. It is recommended that parents and other adults in parental roles foster an atmosphere in which children and adolescents of all ages feel at ease discussing their interactions with technology and voicing their concerns. When young people think that they are being groomed or that they are having improper online interactions, trusting connections provide them with the ability to seek assistance.

This chapter will prepare readers to detect the symptoms of grooming practices, identify possible vulnerabilities in persons, and monitor changes in behaviour that may signal a grooming scenario by the time it is finished. With this information, individuals can take preventative measures to shield themselves and others from the subtle danger posed by cyber grooming.

Understanding the symptoms and warning signs of cyber grooming is essential for determining the nature of any possible dangers and safeguarding oneself and one's loved ones from being exploited online. The following are some frequent warning signals to keep an eye out for, however, the particular manifestations of these symptoms might change depending on the context:

An Excessive Amount of Flattery and Attention: Groomers often use an excessive amount of praise, compliments, and attention to gain their targets' confidence and emotionally manipulate them.

Confidentiality and personal space: Some people who groom others promote confidentiality and insist on having private discussions or encounters that are shielded from the view of other people.

Isolation from Friends and Family Members: Victims may be coerced into isolating themselves from their friends and members of their families, which may result in increasing social isolation.

Emotional Manipulation: People who groom others utilize strategies to manipulate their targets and keep them emotionally reliant on them, such as guilt-tripping and other forms of emotional manipulation.

Under the premise of developing trust, manipulators may pressure their victims to provide personal information by requesting data such as complete names, residences, phone numbers, and information about the schools they attend.

Favours and presents: To keep their targets under control or to "buy" their quiet, groomers sometimes provide favours and presents such as money or gifts of various kinds.

Mood Swings, Anxiety, sadness, and Other Emotional Shifts: As a consequence of the grooming process, victims may experience a range of mood swings, anxiety, sadness, and other emotional shifts.

Isolation from Offline Activities: As people who have been groomed get progressively engaged in an online connection, they may withdraw from offline activities, such as friendships and interests.

Changes in Academic Performance: A decrease in academic performance, an inability to concentrate, or a loss in school attendance are all possible indicators of grooming-related discomfort.

Requests for Sexually Explicit Material: Some groomers may progressively advance the discussion to the point where they ask for or provide sexually explicit material, such as images or videos.

Threats and Blackmail: To exert control over their victims, some groomers may use compromising information they have collected throughout the grooming process to make their victims vulnerable to threats or blackmail.

Manipulation of Trust: People who groom others may take advantage of their targets' trust and vulnerability by seeming as if they are helpful and understanding while progressively increasing the amount of what they want from them.

Unrealistic Promising: Groomers often offer unrealistic promises about the future, such as marriage or financial stability, to keep their targets interested in the relationship.

Isolation from Support Networks: Victims may be convinced to break links with friends, family, or support networks who raise concerns about the online relationship. This may make the victims feel they have no one to turn to for help.

Inconsistent Personal Information Because groomers may supply inconsistent or contradictory information about themselves, it may be difficult to verify that they are who they claim to be.

Forced or coerced actions: In certain instances, groomers may try to pressure victims into acting in a way that makes them uncomfortable or into participating in illegal behaviours.

It is essential to remember that not all contacts online are potentially dangerous; these warning signals should be evaluated within the framework of the particular circumstance. However, suppose you or someone you know comes across several warning signs or experiences discomfort in an online connection. In that case, it is imperative to seek assistance, confide in a reliable source, and contemplate reporting the situation to the appropriate authorities or online platforms. If you or someone you know comes across multiple warning signs or experiences discomfort in a relationship formed online, it is necessary to seek assistance. Put your faith in your gut feelings, prioritise safety, and remember that stopping cyber grooming in its tracks requires prompt action.

FOUR

Digital Platforms and Grooming

Dangers posed by social media platforms, games and online worlds, messaging apps, and online chatrooms

The fourth chapter of "Cyber Grooming: Understanding the Threat in the Digital World" dives into the many digital platforms on which grooming may occur and discusses the unique threats linked with each forum.

Threats Posed by Social Media

The first part of this chapter looks at the dangers of various social media networks. The use of social media to link individuals from different parts of the globe has developed into an essential component of contemporary living. Nonetheless, it also offers a fertile environment for groomers to exploit victims who are unaware that they are being targeted. The reader will develop an understanding of the possible risks associated with oversharing personal information, accepting friend requests from unfamiliar persons, and participating in discussions with unknown people.

The World of Virtual Reality and Video Games

Online games and participation in virtual worlds have amassed a massive following among younger people. These platforms allow users to communicate with one another and immersive experiences. On the other hand, they bring their particular dangers. This chapter investigates how groomers might take advantage of the social features of online gaming, especially those games that combine voice chat and text messaging. The reader will come away with a better awareness of the significance of online gaming safety and the steps they may take to safeguard themselves or their children.

Apps for instant messaging and online chatrooms

Another primary focus of this chapter is on the use of chatrooms and messaging applications. These platforms provide those who engage in grooming the ability to remain anonymous while still providing direct access to prospective victims. The chapter warns its readers against the perils of striking up discussions with strangers, divulging private information, and allowing oneself to be tricked by those putting on false identities. In addition, it offers instructions on recognising and reporting suspicious activity in online chat situations.

Awareness and Education are Necessary

The necessity of knowledge and vigilance is emphasized several times throughout Chapter 4. It is strongly recommended that readers educate both themselves and their children on the possible dangers that are linked with using a variety of different digital platforms. It is essential to have a solid understanding of the various threats offered by these platforms to take the necessary safeguards and promote online safety.

When they have finished reading this chapter, the audience will be completely aware of the hazards connected with various digital platforms and how groomers use the situations in which these platforms are used. Individuals armed with this information can make educated judgments regarding the nature of their online contacts and take preventative measures to safeguard themselves and the people they care about from the dangers posed by cyber grooming.

A report suggests:

The advent of the digital age has fundamentally altered how we interact and communicate with one another. Internet use has several advantages, but it also brings several new difficulties, most notably in protecting one's privacy online. One of the most problematic problems is known as cyber grooming, which occurs when persons, most of the time harm, use digital platforms to target and influence vulnerable individuals, most often children and teenagers.

The purpose of this paper is to investigate the function that various online platforms play in enabling cyber grooming, illuminating the unique risks connected with these platforms, and supplying insights into the strategies that groomers use.

Platforms for Social Media People use social media platforms extensively to interact with friends and share their experiences. However, they are also susceptible to being used as hunting grounds by groomers. The following are some of the elements that are highlighted in the report:

Requests for Friendship: To get access to the profiles of young people, groomers often make friend requests to them, pretending to be their classmates or using fake identities.

Private Messages: Predators utilize the private message capabilities of social media platforms to engage their victims out of public view, where they have more power to influence and control their prey.

Sharing of Information: Grooming may occur when victims unwittingly reveal personal information in their profiles or postings, such as the names of their schools, places, or hobbies. This makes them more vulnerable to being targeted.

Gaming Online and Participating in Virtual Worlds Both online gaming and participating in virtual worlds have seen a surge in popularity recently, particularly among younger people. While they may be a source of amusement and possibilities for social engagement, they also provide some novel dangers:

Voice Chat and Messages: Because certain games offer voice chat and messages, groomers have direct access to children while playing such games.

Gifts and Virtual money: Some manipulators may utilize in-game cash or skills to win their victims' confidence and exploit that trust.

Anonymity: Groomers can disguise their real identities because of the anonymity granted by some online gaming platforms.

Chatrooms and Messaging applications: Both chatrooms and messaging applications provide quick and easy ways to connect with others. Sadly, they also present possibilities for exploiters to take advantage of susceptible individuals:

Groomers can conceal their identities by using chat applications, where they may establish anonymous accounts that make it harder to determine their genuine motives.

Private Conversations: Because victims may feel more at ease revealing personal information with an unknown person in a private chatroom or during a one-on-one discussion, grooming may occur more quickly in these settings.

Deceptive Personas: To exert emotional control over their prey, groomers often assume the role of sympathetic or understanding persons.

Education and Awareness: The significance of education and awareness as preventative measures against grooming on digital platforms is emphasized in the research. The following courses of action are suggested in the report:

Programs for Digital Literacy: To educate kids about the dangers of grooming, other forms of inappropriate online conduct, and online safety, schools should include digital literacy programs in their curricula.

Advice for Parents and Guardians: Parents and guardians should actively participate in their children's online activities, teach their children about the risks that may be involved, and keep the lines of communication open.

Tools for Online Safety The use of online safety tools, such as parental control software and privacy settings, is strongly encouraged throughout the study to enhance protection further.

In this day and age of the digital revolution, digital platforms have rapidly become an indispensable component of our everyday lives. These platforms provide us with both possibilities and threats. It is vital to take preventative measures against cyber grooming, such as being aware of the risks connected with the platforms in question and being cautious about one's online behaviour. We can work together to make the internet a more secure place for everyone if we educate people, parents, and communities on how to use it safely.

This research is intended to serve as a rallying cry, asking people and authorities to prioritise online safety, establish comprehensive awareness programs, and implement effective measures to prevent cyber grooming on digital platforms.

In the following chapters, we will continue to investigate real-life tales, different preventative techniques, and the role of education and support in the fight against cyberbullying. Our goal is to provide people and communities with the knowledge necessary to traverse the digital world securely.

FIVE

THE EMOTIONAL TOLL

Psychological Manipulation, Trauma, and Long-Term Effects of Cyber Grooming

Chapter 5 of "Cyber Grooming: Understanding the Threat in the Digital World" delves into the profound emotional toll that cyber grooming can inflict upon its victims. Groomers employ tactics designed to manipulate and control their targets, resulting in psychological and emotional consequences.

Psychological Manipulation The chapter begins by exploring the psychological manipulation techniques used by groomers. These tactics can include gaslighting, emotional blackmail, and threats. Readers will gain insights into how groomers erode their victims' self-esteem, sense of agency, and critical thinking skills, making it increasingly challenging for victims to break free from their influence.

Trauma and Emotional Scars Victims of cyber grooming often experience significant trauma and emotional scars. The chapter delves into the emotional turmoil endured by victims, which can include anxiety, depression, post-traumatic stress disorder (PTSD), and other lasting psychological effects. Readers will gain an understanding of the depth of suffering experienced by survivors.

The Long-Term Effects Cyber grooming's impact extends far beyond the immediate grooming experience. This chapter examines the long-term effects that victims may have, such as trust issues, difficulties forming healthy relationships, and challenges establishing boundaries. Readers will gain insights into the enduring consequences of cyber grooming on a person's overall well-being.

Support and Healing Throughout Chapter 5, help and healing are emphasized. Victims of cyber grooming require empathetic and professional assistance to overcome the emotional trauma they have endured. The chapter discusses the role of therapy, counselling, and support networks in helping survivors heal and recover.

By the end of this chapter, readers will have a comprehensive understanding of the emotional toll that cyberbullying inflicts on its victims. Recognizing the psychological manipulation and trauma associated with grooming is crucial for identifying and assisting survivors on their journey to recovery.

The victims of cyber grooming are left with significant psychological and emotional wounds, making it a severe and pervasive threat in the digital world. This paper investigates the complex web of psychological manipulation that is used by groomers, the painful experiences that victims go through, and the long-lasting repercussions that cyber grooming has on people.

Psychological Manipulation Cyber grooming often starts with the victim being subjected to various psychological manipulation techniques that have been meticulously crafted to both control and exploit them. The following are some of the elements that are highlighted in the report:

Gaslighting is a method that groomers use to influence their victims into questioning their perceptions, reality, and instincts. This allows the groomer to acquire control over the victims' feelings and behaviour.

Emotional Blackmail: Groomers use emotional blackmail by threatening to reveal sensitive information or explicit material that victims may have told while being groomed. This tactic is used to coerce victims into sharing information.

Isolation: Victims are tricked into separating themselves from friends, family, and support networks, which makes them more reliant on the groomer for emotional validation and support. This is accomplished by isolating the victim from friends, family, and support networks.

A Wide Variety of Traumatic Experiences and Emotional Scars Cyber grooming exacts a significant mental and emotional toll on its victims, leaving them with a host of traumatic experiences and emotional scars. The following topics are explored in depth in the report:

Anxiety and Depression: As a result of the emotional manipulation, victims of grooming often feel increased levels of both anxiety and depression. This hurts their mental health.

Some victims acquire post-traumatic stress disorder (PTSD) as a result of the upsetting nature of the grooming experience, which may cause them to have flashbacks, nightmares, and emotional anguish.

Problems with confidence: Because grooming causes victims' trust in others to be shattered, it is difficult for them to build healthy relationships, and it creates an ongoing dread of being betrayed.

Setting Boundaries: Victims often have difficulties setting boundaries, and they may have trouble saying "no" or recognizing when they are in toxic relationships. Victims also often struggle to identify when they are in harmful relationships.

Impacts That Last A Lifetime The influence of cyber grooming goes much beyond the immediate experience of grooming; instead, it leaves implications that last a lifetime and impact many facets of a person's life. The following long-term effects are specifically highlighted in the report:

Problems with Trust and Difficulties in Defining Boundaries May Make It Difficult for Victims to Develop and Maintain Healthy Relationships. Victims may find it challenging to develop and maintain healthy relationships owing to trust problems and difficulties in defining boundaries.

Isolation from Society: One of the long-term repercussions is often the victim's withdrawal from social activities and connections, which may lead to social isolation.

Emotional Resilience: Victims may have difficulty building their emotional resilience, making it difficult to deal with everyday life's challenges.

Healing and Recovery: The need for professional counselling and treatment and support networks is emphasized in the study as a means by which survivors may be assisted on their journey toward recovery and healing.

The fact that cyber grooming may cause psychological manipulation and trauma, as well as long-term impacts, is a glaring reminder of the essential need to battle this digital threat. The lack of early intervention, support, and education cannot be overstated in light of the emotional toll that is inflicted on victims of grooming by having this understanding.

This study is meant to serve as a call to action, asking authorities, communities, and people to prioritize care for survivors, increase awareness about the emotional costs of grooming, and work together to build a safer digital environment for everyone. We may take measures to avoid the disastrous repercussions that cyber grooming can have on persons and their well-being if we first acknowledge the long-lasting impacts of the practice.

In the subsequent chapters, we will continue to explore real-life stories, prevention strategies, and the role of education and support in combating cyberbullying. Ultimately, our goal is to empower individuals and communities to navigate the digital world safely and support those who have experienced the devastating effects of cyberbullying.

SIX

REAL LIFE STORIES

Personal Accounts of Grooming, Lessons Learned from Survivors, The Importance of Sharing Stories

Chapter 6 of "Cyber Grooming: Understanding the Threat in the Digital World" takes a poignant turn as it presents real-life stories of individuals who have experienced cyber grooming. These personal accounts serve as powerful narratives that shed light on the devastating impact of grooming and impart invaluable lessons.

Personal Accounts of Grooming In this chapter, readers will encounter firsthand testimonies from survivors who bravely share their experiences. These personal accounts provide insight into the deceptive tactics used by groomers, the emotional turmoil endured by victims, and the challenges they faced in breaking free from the influence of their groomers.

Source: https://mindthegapalways.in/tag/cyber-violence/

Lessons Learned from Survivors of cyber grooming often emerge from their ordeals with newfound wisdom and resilience. This chapter highlights the lessons learned by survivors, including the importance of trust, resilience, and the significance of seeking help. These lessons serve as beacons of hope and inspiration for others facing similar challenges.

The Importance of Sharing Stories Chapter 6 underscores the vital role of sharing stories in raising awareness and fostering empathy. By sharing their experiences, survivors find healing and closure and contribute to a collective effort to combat cyberbullying. The chapter discusses the impact of survivor narratives on increasing public awareness and driving change.

A Call to Action Throughout this chapter, readers are invited to reflect on the stories they encounter and consider our collective responsibility in addressing cyber grooming. The reports serve as a call to action, encouraging individuals, families, educators, and communities to combat this digital menace proactively.

Source: https://www.timesnownews.com/bengaluru/
bengaluru-police-spread-awareness-about-cyber-grooming-
know-what-it-is-article-94964733

Source: https://www.timesnownews.com/bengaluru/
bengaluru-police-spread-awareness-about-cyber-grooming-
know-what-it-is-article-94964733

By the end of this chapter, readers will have gained a deeper understanding of the human stories behind cyber grooming, the resilience of survivors, and the importance of sharing experiences to drive change. These stories serve as a powerful reminder of the urgent need to take action against this pervasive threat.

Source: https://tullimbar-p.schools.nsw.gov.au/news/
2023/10/wake-up-wednesday---online-grooming.html

In the subsequent chapters, we will continue to explore prevention strategies, reporting and legal measures, support and recovery, and the broader initiatives required to create a safer digital world for all.

SEVEN

PRECAUTIONS FOR CYBER GROOMING: UNDERSTANDING THE THREAT IN THE DIGITAL WORLD

Protecting yourself and your loved ones from the threat of cyber grooming requires awareness, vigilance, and proactive measures.

Here are some crucial precautions to consider:

.

Educate Yourself and Your Family:

- Stay informed about the tactics used by groomers, the signs of grooming behaviour, and the potential dangers of online interactions.

- Educate your family, especially children and adolescents, about the risks and realities of cyber grooming. Encourage open communication about online experiences.

Maintain Privacy:

- Be cautious about sharing personal information on public forums and social media, such as full names, addresses, phone numbers, school names, and birthdates.

-

Review and adjust privacy settings on social media platforms to limit the visibility of personal information to strangers.

- **Use Strong, Unique Passwords:**

  - *Create strong, unique passwords for online accounts, and consider using a reputable password manager to keep track of them.*

    - *Enable two-factor authentication (2FA) wherever possible to add an extra layer of security to your accounts.*

- **Exercise Caution with Social Media:**

- *Avoid accepting friend or connection requests from individuals you don't know personally.*

  - *Be sceptical of unsolicited messages or requests for personal information on social media platforms.*

- *Monitor Online Activity:*

  - *Keep an eye on the online activities of your children and adolescents. Know who they are communicating with and what platforms they are using.*

- *Encourage them to report any suspicious or uncomfortable interactions to a trusted adult.*

- *Secure Devices and Software:*

  - *Keep your devices and software up to date with the latest security patches.*

- *Install reputable antivirus and anti-malware software to protect against potential threats.*

Teach Critical Thinking:

○

Help children and adolescents develop critical thinking skills. Encourage them to question the authenticity of online information and the motives of individuals they interact with.

•

Establish Boundaries:

○

Set clear boundaries regarding online behaviour and screen time. Encourage a healthy balance between digital and offline activities.

•

Discuss the importance of reporting any online encounters that make them uncomfortable.

•

Online Gaming Safety:

○

If your child engages in online gaming, educate them about the potential risks and the importance of not sharing personal information during gaming sessions.

○

Consider using parental controls and privacy settings on gaming consoles and platforms.

•

Encourage Reporting:

•

Create an environment where children and adolescents feel safe reporting any incidents of cyber grooming to a trusted adult.

○

If you suspect grooming or encounter suspicious behaviour, report it to the appropriate authorities and the platform in question.

•

Support and Communication:

○

Foster open communication within your family, emphasizing trust and understanding. Encourage conversations about online experiences without judgment.

Stay Informed:

Keep up to date with the latest trends and technologies in the digital world. Awareness is a powerful tool in protecting against online threats.

Remember that cyber grooming can happen to anyone, regardless of age, gender, or background. By taking these precautions and staying vigilant, you can significantly reduce the risk of falling victim to this insidious threat and help create a safer digital environment for yourself and your loved ones.

Building digital resiliency, providing parental guidance, and implementing school programs are all aspects of prevention and education.

Prevention and education are our most powerful friends in the fight against cyber grooming, which takes place via the internet. If we pursue these many learning routes, we can arm ourselves and the next generation with the knowledge and abilities to navigate the digital environment securely. Building digital resiliency, parental advice and communication, and school programs and curricula are the three pillars of prevention and education discussed in this chapter.

Developing a Digital Defense Strategy

Digital resilience is the armour people wear to guard themselves from risks posed by the internet, and it is an essential component of our protection when using the internet. It requires a solid grasp of the digital world, identifying possible threats, and gaining the skills to react successfully. The following are some of the most critical aspects of developing digital resilience:

To raise awareness, individuals should be encouraged to remain current on the newest internet hazards and trends. The first step in ensuring your safety in the ever-changing digital ecosystem is understanding that landscape.

Critical Thinking: Teach individuals the skills necessary to evaluate the reliability of online material and the intents of the people they engage with.

Etiquette Online: Stress the need to maintain proper online etiquette, which includes maintaining courteous communication, responsibly sharing material, and avoiding engaging in cyberbullying.

Secure Behaviors Encourage people to engage in safe online behaviours, such as selecting strong passwords, maintaining up-to-date software, and exercising caution before exposing personal information.

Counselling and Conversation with One's Parents

Source: https://www.nottinghamgirlsacademy.org/
page/?title=Grooming&pid=129

Their children's safety when using the internet is significantly impacted by the actions of their parents and other caregivers. Effective parental direction and communication may help establish a setting that is both secure and open for addressing events that occur online:

Encourage children to communicate with you in an open way that does not include judgment. Encourage them to discuss their experiences, concerns, and questions about online time.

Defining limits: Defining and establishing explicit norms and limitations is essential when engaging in activities online. Talk about setting boundaries on the time spent in front of screens, selecting acceptable websites and applications, and the significance of reporting unsettling encounters.

Educate One Another: Have family discussions on how to be safe while using the internet. Investigate the available internet resources and follow the safety advice as a group.

Utilize Parental Controls When supervising and limiting younger children's participation in online activities, it's a good idea to utilize parental control tools and software.

The Programs and Curriculum of the Schools

When it comes to teaching pupils about the digital world and the risks that may be associated with it, schools play a crucial role. Comprehensive educational programs and curriculums that are focused on internet safety must be implemented in schools:

Literacy in the Digital Age: Educate children on how to browse the internet securely, recognize grooming habits, and react appropriately by including programs that teach digital literacy into the school's regular curriculum.

Raise awareness about cybersecurity by emphasizing the need to use robust passwords, identify and avoid phishing efforts, and safeguard personal information.

Emotional Well-Being: Address the emotional effect of online encounters and provide students with strategies to deal with possible grooming scenarios, cyberbullying, and harassment.

Establishing Clear Reporting Mechanisms: It is essential to provide transparent reporting mechanisms within the school environment so kids may report any online occurrences or concerns privately.

We can establish a complete defence against cyber grooming by actively promoting digital resilience, supporting open communication within families, and incorporating online safety into schools' curricula. Education and prevention are not merely tactics but the cornerstones upon which we may construct a safer digital environment for ourselves and future generations.